LATINOS IN BASEBALL

Tino Martinez

John A. Torres

Mitchell Lane Publishers, Inc.
P.O. Box 619
Bear, Delaware 19701

LATINOS IN BASEBALL

Tino Martinez   Bobby Bonilla   Roberto Alomar   Pedro Martinez
Moises Alou   Sammy Sosa   Ivan Rodriguez   Manny Ramirez
Ramon Martinez   Alex Rodriguez   Vinny Castilla   Bernie Williams

Library of Congress Cataloging-in-Publication Data

Torres, John A.
    Tino Martinez / John A. Torres.
        p. cm. — (Latinos in baseball)
    Includes index.
    Summary: Presents a biography of the professional baseball player, from his childhood in Tampa, Florida, to his successful career with the New York Yankees.
    ISBN 1-883845-82-3 (lib. bdg.)
    1. Martinez, Tino, 1967-   —Juvenile literature. 2. Baseball players—United States—Biography—Juvenile literature. [1. Martinez, Tino, 1967-   . 2. Baseball players. 3. Hispanic Americans—Biography.] I. Title. II. Series.
GV865.M357T67 1999
796.357' 092—dc21
[b]
                                                                                    98-48049
                                                                                        CIP
                                                                                         AC

About the Author: John A. Torres is a newspaper reporter for the Poughkeepsie Journal in New York. He has written eleven sports biographies, including *Greg Maddux* (Lerner), *Hakeem Olajuwon* (Enslow), and *Darryl Strawberry* (Enslow). He lives in Fishkill, New York with his wife and two children. When not writing, John likes to spend his time fishing, coaching Little League Baseball, and spending time with his family.

Photo Credits: cover: ©1998 New York Yankees; pp. 4 Kirby Lee/Marin and Assoc.; p. 7, 10 ©1998 New York Yankees; p.32 A. Kaye/Allsport; p. 36 Ken Levine/Allsport; pp. 38, 42 AP Photo; p. 47 ©1998 New York Yankees; p. 55 Reuters/Sue Ogrocki/Archive Photos; pp. 50, 51, 62 © 1998 New York Yankees; p. 56 Globe Photos; p. 60 Craig Melvin/Allsport

Acknowledgments: This story has been thoroughly researched and checked for accuracy. To the best of our knowledge, it represents a true story.

Dedication: Baseball, like family history, gets passed on from generation to generation. It is the easiest, most pure thing that gets passed from grandfather to father to son. This book is dedicated to my son, Daniel, with whom I can never play enough baseball, and to my father, Rico, and my father-in-law, Frank, who love to talk about baseball almost as much as I do.—John A. Torres

TABLE OF CONTENTS

CHAPTER ONE
Hard Work

The list of great New York Yankee first basemen is an impressive one. There was Hall of Famer Lou Gehrig, the "Iron Horse" who belted 493 home runs during the 1920s and '30s. There was three-time All-Star Joe Pepitone, who played great baseball for some very bad Yankee teams in the 1960s. There was Chris Chambliss, who had a pennant-winning home run against the Kansas City Royals in 1976. Then there was the 1980s fan favorite, the Captain, Don Mattingly, who patrolled first base for 13 years at Yankee Stadium. Mattingly was one of the most-loved players ever to wear Yankee pinstripes.

When the Yankees traded highly rated young players Sterling Hitchcock and Russell Davis for Seattle Mariner first baseman Tino Martinez in 1995, the pressure was squarely on Tino's shoulders to succeed. After all, he was replacing a legend on a team that simply demands greatness.

Most players do not like to be traded. But it was a magical day for Tino, and it could not have turned out any better. Tino was traded to the Yankees on December 7, 1995, which happened to be his 28th birthday. A few hours after the trade, Tino was there to help his wife, Marie, give birth to their daughter, Victoria. Then, the Yankees awarded Tino with a new five-year, $20 million contract. The contract meant that Tino would never have to worry about money again. A new team, a new baby, and a new contract, all on the same day, his birthday.

"This is one of the greatest days of my life," Tino said on a conference call to reporters that night. "My head is spinning."

Tino had heard about the pressure of playing for the New York Yankees. He also knew he was replacing a legend in Mattingly, who had announced his retirement because of a bad back. In Seattle, Tino did not have a lot of pressure playing for the Mariners, since they had All-Stars Ken Griffey Jr., Jay Buhner, and Edgar Martinez already in their lineup. The Yankees had a good team too, but they would expect Tino to be a main part of their offense.

"It won't be easy to replace Don Mattingly, but in Tino Martinez, we think we have one of the brightest young first basemen in baseball today," Yankee general manager Bob Watson said after the trade.

Tino was not worried about the pressure. He knows there is only one way to accomplish great things in life: hard work.

"I'm not going to think about Don Mattingly on the field," Martinez said. "It's all part of replacing a legend. I've always believed that the answer to your problems is working harder."

Tino did not have to convince himself or his teammates. They all knew he was a very talented player. But the fans were another matter. They would be watching Tino closely to make sure he knew that Mattingly was their favorite.

Don Mattingly was a legendary New York Yankee first baseman for 13 years.

The previous season, for Seattle, Tino batted .293, belted 31 homers, and drove in 111 runs. If he came close to those numbers as a Yankee, he would become a fan favorite.

Yankee outfielder Paul O'Neill became one of Tino's best friends on the team, and one of his biggest supporters. "I hope he doesn't put the burden on himself to be Don Mattingly," O'Neill told *The New York Times*. "Don Mattingly has a history with the Yankees; Tino is just starting his."

Tino did not get off to a fast start as a Yankee, and the Mattingly fans really began to get on Tino's back—even though Tino tried hard to do all the right things. Tino's number had always been 23, but as a Yankee he asked for 24, since Mattingly had worn 23. Tino had grown up a Yankee fan, and Mattingly and Ryne Sandberg of the Chicago Cubs were always his favorite players. Sandberg also wore number 23.

"I grew up a Yankee fan in the Reggie Jackson era when they had Lou Piniella, Chris Chambliss, those guys," Tino said after the trade. Piniella had grown up in Tino's neighborhood and was very close friends with Tino's family.

After the first three weeks of the season, Tino was really struggling: he was batting only .196 and did not get a base hit over his first 16 at-bats at Yankee

Stadium. Some Yankee fans began to taunt and boo him, and some even chanted for Mattingly.

The fans were waiting to see the Tino Martinez who just a few months before had helped the Mariners come from two games behind and win a playoff series against their Yankees. New York had taken a 2-0 lead in the best-of-five series and seemed ready for a three-game sweep. They had been leading Seattle 1-0 in the fifth inning when Tino came to bat against Yankee ace Jack McDowell. With a man on base, McDowell did not want to throw any wild pitches, so he threw Tino a fastball. Tino crushed it, deep over the right-field fence, giving the Mariners a 2-1 lead. The fans in Seattle cheered like crazy. The place became so loud that it seemed to rattle the Yankee pitcher. The very next inning, Tino laced a bases-loaded single to help put the game away. His timely hitting helped spark his teammates, who won the next two games and took the series three games to two.

"McDowell was pitching a superb game when Tino got us on board," Seattle manager Lou Piniella said. "That homer was what we needed. He really got us and the crowd going."

Tino was still happy that he had been traded to the Yankees, but he also realized that this was the toughest stretch that his short career had seen. He felt

In 1995, Tino was ranked first in fielding among American League first basemen.

that every mistake he made was being magnified. He also was not used to getting booed. But Tino kept working hard. He took extra batting practice and showed up early for instruction. He knew that with hard work, he would get back to his usual self.

At first, the hard work seemed to backfire. Tino was trying too hard: he was pressing instead of playing naturally. He ended up batting .244 for the month of April, and much lower at home. Tino still refused to blame his slow start on Mattingly's shadow.

"It had nothing to do with Mattingly," he said. "I tried to do too much when I first got there [to New York]. I tried to impress everybody: the new coaching staff, the fans, everybody. I was just overdoing everything."

Tino continued to work hard and not put so much pressure on himself. He also got a word of comfort from an unexpected source. Tino had telephoned his agent, Jim Krivacs, for some advice. But Krivacs put someone else on the phone to talk to Tino. It was Don Mattingly.

"Don't give up. Just keep plugging away," Mattingly told Tino. "You'll be fine."

Those words seemed to work magic for Tino because a few nights later he belted a three-run home run in the seventh inning, which turned out to be the game-winning hit in a victory over the Baltimore Orioles at Camden Yards. That hit helped put the Yankees in first place. The very next night, Tino smashed a grand slam in the 15th inning, once again lifting the Yankees to victory.

On June 16, Tino drove in three runs against tough Cleveland Indians pitcher Dennis Martinez. It gave Tino a total of 49 RBIs (runs batted in) just 65 games into the season. It was a noteworthy accomplishment, because Mattingly had had only 49 RBIs for the entire season just a year before. It took Tino only 65 games to do what it had taken Mattingly 128 games to do. Tino finally felt as if he belonged.

"They'll never forget Don Mattingly here and I don't want them to," Tino said. "I want the fans to support me and support this team. I've gotten that. That's a really good feeling. To feel like I belong here is great."

He finally won the fans over to his side and has been belting game-winning hits and home runs for the Yanks ever since. Hard work and patience helped Tino through a tough time.

But Tino has always been used to hard work. Growing up, hard work was part of his everyday life.

CHAPTER 2
"I Want to Be a Baseball Player"

Constantino (Tino) Martinez was born on December 7, 1967, in Tampa Bay, Florida. He was named after his grandfather, who also lived in Tampa. From childhood, Tino saw the rewards of hard work. His grandfather had advanced himself from being an employee at the Villazon Cigar Company in Tampa to becoming the owner. Tino's father, Rene Sr., the general manager of the factory, never missed a day of work.

"Hard work is a lesson that I learned from my father," Tino said. "No one worked harder than he did."

During summer and other vacations from school, Tino and his brothers would spend their mornings working at the factory as well. Tino started when he was ten years old with his older brother, Rene Jr. A few years later, their younger brother, Tony, would join them. The average day would start at 6:30 in the morning with a phone call from Tino's father. He would have already been working at the factory, which was only a block from the Martinez home, for about three hours. A shipment of tobacco would have arrived, probably from Honduras, and it would have had to have been unloaded.

Tino's mother, Sylvia, would wake the boys and they would run off to the factory. There, they would help unload the 100-pound crates of tobacco. They would also help out in the fumigation chambers, and they would arrange the tobacco in the sorting room, which was usually hotter than the hot Florida air outside.

Tino can still hear his father's favorite expression ringing in his ears: "Hard work never hurt anybody."

Tino's father was trying to teach his boys a lesson. While he never came out and said exactly what he was trying to do, Tino knew that he had a clear message. The message was that if you stay in school and work hard, then you can make something of yourself. It is a lesson that Tino still carries with him today. "It taught me to work hard as a player," he says.

It did not take long for Tino to decide what he wanted to do with his life. By the time he was five years old, Tino and his older brother, Rene Jr., were both huge baseball fans. Tino's dad was a big, strong man, 240 pounds, who had been a football star at Tampa High School. He did not know a lot about baseball, but in order to please his children, Rene studied the game and learned a lot. He wanted to be able to instruct them properly. He also began taking them to watch the Cincinnati Reds in spring training. Many of the major-league baseball teams travel to Florida in the early spring to practice in the warm weather.

At the age of five, Tino saw something that would change his life forever. Cincinnati Reds slugger George Foster was hitting baseballs off a tee into a fence. Many times, baseball players will hit balls off tees to work on their swing. Foster hit ball after ball into this fence. It looked as if he were trying to put a hole in the fence.

Although he was not a baseball player, Tino's father was very involved with sports. Years after playing football, he became involved in neighborhood activities. He served as a member of the Tampa Sports Authority, which oversaw athletic activities in the city. He was also a member of the Civil Service Board.

Tino and his family are of Spanish descent. His great-great-grandparents were from Spain.

Tino grew up on Kathleen Street in West Tampa, which is, ironically, only minutes away from the Yankees' new spring training stadium. One of his neighbors in Tampa was former major-league player and Seattle Mariner manager Lou Piniella. Piniella's family was also from Spain.

"I've known Tino's family since I was a kid myself," Piniella said. "I grew up on the same block on St. Conrad Street with his dad, Rene."

Piniella and Rene played football together as kids. But while Rene excelled at football, Lou concentrated on baseball. When Lou was about 13 years old, he moved across town to Cordelia Street, where he lived right across from a playground. On the other side of the playground lived a girl named Sylvia, who would become Tino's mother.

"I've known that family forever," Piniella laughs.

Soon after watching Foster pound baseballs off the tee, Tino declared to his mom and dad and everyone else who would listen: "When I grow up, I want to be a baseball player."

Tino thought it was great to watch what Foster was doing. Soon after that, his parents bought him a batting tee and Tino began to hit baseballs in the backyard. His parents were very supportive of his love of baseball. They enrolled him and Rene Jr. in Little League and would encourage them at every opportunity.

Rene Sr. constantly told the boys that if they worked hard enough and if they believed hard enough, they could make the major leagues.

By the time he was eight years old, Tino already had a confidence about him that is usually reserved for someone much older. He was so confident, in fact, that he decided he wanted to try switch-hitting. A switch-hitter bats from both sides of the plate. His experiment was successful. Tino homered batting left-handed and right-handed. Although he hit a home run batting right-handed, his father convinced him to concentrate on batting from his usual left-handed side. It is very hard to become a good switch-hitter. Tino's father wanted him to just play his natural way.

Many times Tino and Rene Jr. would play on the same teams. This made it easy for Tino's parents to pick which team to root for. Tino seemed like a natural on the baseball field. He had grace and presence and was soon the star of the league. Other kids looked up to him.

When he was 12 years old, Tino had an unbelievable Little League season. He belted 25 home runs—in only 24 games! When it was discovered that Tino had been weight lifting to increase his upper body strength, it began an epidemic. Just about every kid in the league began lifting weights.

At the age of 13, Tino began to mimic George Foster's practice habits. He set the batting tee up near a fence in his backyard and soon began crushing ball after ball into it, trying to put the ball through the fence. It became a near obsession. After doing his homework or his chores, Tino would take a bucket of balls and hit them off the tee, trying to perfect his swing. He would keep his back elbow raised and his wrists low, trying to minimize his motions. The more motion you have in your swing and approach, the more chance you have that something will go wrong. Tino liked to keep it simple.

"If he was bored and had nothing to do, he'd go back to the tee and hit," his brother Rene said.

Tino would call practice his work and the backyard his office. He would yell to his mother, "I love my office outside!" She would answer: "You sure do."

Hitting baseballs off a tee is something that Tino still does. Getting into that habit has helped to produce one of the sweetest baseball swings in the game today. Tino rarely looks awkward while taking a swing. Some people liken his stroke to that of Hall of Famer Ted Williams. Williams is known as one of the best to have ever played the game.

While Tino played in Little League, his parents secretly started a scrapbook for him. His name was mentioned often in the local newspapers because he was such a good player. His parents would clip the articles and paste them into the book. But they did not tell Tino about it.

"They never wanted me to let success go to my head," Tino said. But it was hard for him not to know just how good he was. Everybody who saw him play told him so.

Nothing demonstrates better the impact that Tino had on his teams than his high-school baseball experience. While most high-school baseball players hope to make it to the state finals at least once, Tino had the distinction of leading two seperate schools to the finals. Tino and his sweet swing led Tampa Catholic High School to the Florida State Championship in 1982. He later transferred to Jefferson High School, a public school in Tampa. He led them to the Florida State Finals in 1985.

In Florida, high-school baseball is competitive and year round. Because of the warm weather there, the schools play two seasons: a fall schedule and a spring schedule. Up North, most schools can play only a spring season.

Tampa is also known as one of the few cities in the United States where interest in high-school baseball is stronger than interest in high-school football or basketball. There are also a lot of youth programs there that have very dedicated and experienced coaches. In fact, *Sports Illustrated* reported that no other U.S. city produces as many good baseball players as Tampa.

The 1985 state finalist team, the Jefferson Dragons, had Tino playing first base and Luis Gonzalez playing second base. Gonzalez would later play for the Houston Astros. Another major-league All-Star who played for Jefferson High School is Fred McGriff, who has enjoyed success with the San Diego Padres and the Atlanta Braves.

Jefferson's rival, Hillsborough High School, also in Tampa, has produced such major-leaguers as Dwight Gooden, Gary Sheffield, and retired pitcher Floyd Youmans. Other players from Tampa include longtime player and manager Lou Piniella; Dave Magadan, who is Piniella's cousin; Derek Bell; Carl Everett; and Wade Boggs. Major-league manager Tony La Russa and All-Star first baseman Steve Garvey are also from Tampa.

Tino's high-school coach, Pop Cuesta, has coached at Jefferson since 1960. He is very proud of the legacy his city has produced.

"If you sketch out an all-Tampa team, you've got batting champs and plenty of World Series rings," Cuesta told *Sports Illustrated.* "That team would be very competitive in the major leagues today."

Other players agree.

"It's special being from Tampa," Sheffield says. "It's like a fraternity. When you're from Tampa, people know you're a serious ballplayer."

"When I was growing up, baseball was a top priority, not football or soccer," said Gonzalez.

Tampa's great success at turning out quality baseball players can also be traced to the city's diverse ethnic makeup. Tampa is truly an ethnic melting pot, boasting a huge Cuban population, a large African-American population, as well as a large white population.

Ybor City, a neighborhood in Tampa, is so diverse that it has the only newspaper in the country that is printed in three languages. It is printed in English, Spanish, and Italian. Ybor is where most of the cigar factories are located.

Tampa Bay got its own major-league baseball team in 1998 when the Devil Rays took the field for the first time. Many felt that the team had a real advantage in scouting the rich talent pool in its own city.

Tino's older brother, Rene, was a good baseball player also. Although he was not as good as Tino, he was still the starting shortstop for the University of Tampa. He did not pursue baseball as a profession, however. During his senior year at Jefferson High School, Tino was followed around at every game by scouts and coaches from major colleges as well as from major-league teams. He received several scholarship offers to play baseball for big-name colleges. It was clear by now that Tino would get a free education and have a chance at making it to the major leagues.

In fact, the Boston Red Sox selected Tino in the June 1985 amateur draft with their third selection. They wanted to sign him right away and assign him to the minor leagues, where he could work his way up to the pros. Every major-league baseball team has a minor-league system in which young players can mature and learn the game better.

Tino and his family talked it over and they thought it best for Tino to go to college. He would get an education and he would not risk getting lost in the minor-league shuffle. On a college team, Tino would get the attention he needed to become a better player.

Tino, however, was not interested in going to a big-name school. He wanted to stay close to home, and he also wanted to play with his brother. His father wanted Tino to go to a major school. After all, he argued, the major leagues look at those schools before they ever look at the University of Tampa.

But Lou Piniella assured Tino's father that it did not matter where Tino went to school. "If he's good enough," he said, "they'll find him anywhere."

So Tino went to the University of Tampa. It did not turn out to be a mistake.

CHAPTER 3
All-American

I t certainly was not a mistake for Tino to play base-ball for the University of Tampa. He was an instant success on the field and in the classroom. His parents truly believed that Tino would make it to the major leagues one day, but they did not want him to neglect his studies. Tino worked hard at both.

On the field, Tino attracted a lot of attention. Still working hard by hitting balls off tees, Tino continued to have a perfect swing. He also continued to pound the baseball. He had grown and now was the ideal height and weight for a baseball player. Tino topped six feet and hovered around 200 pounds.

Tino's college coach, Ken Dominguez, had followed Tino's progress from Little League through high school. He was excited about being able to coach him.

"I remember telling someone when Tino was 12 years old that if everything goes its course, he'll play in the major leagues someday," he told *The New York Times*. "He had a presence about him. He was special."

Rene Sr. was still a big influence on Tino. He constantly preached to his son about hard work. He also kept telling him that he would make the major leagues if he believed in himself.

"I was always a good hitter," Tino told *The New York Times.* "But I didn't have speed or a great arm. I had to work extra hard to convince people that I could be a major-leaguer."

Tino played first base for the University of Tampa, which is a Division II school. Most of the major colleges play in a tougher league, Division I. Tino was named a Division II All-American all three years that he played for them. Being named All-American is an honor reserved for the best college athletes. He was also named an Academic All-American. This meant that he excelled in the classroom as well as on the baseball field.

During his three years at the University of Tampa, Tino set college records that still stand today. His career records there include best batting average, .398; most home runs, 54; and most runs batted in, 222. Tino was so good that he was named first baseman on The Sporting News All-American team in 1988. It is very rare that a player from a Division II college team receives such an honor.

The St. Louis Cardinals were one of many teams that sent scouts to the University of Tampa to watch Tino play baseball. Impressed, they were hoping to draft him. The Cardinals sent Marty Maier, their assistant scouting director, many times to see Tino. One time, he watched Tino hit three home runs in a single game. He hit one to left field, one to right field, and one to straightaway center field.

By June of 1988, it was clear that Tino would make it to the major leagues. In fact, the Seattle Mariners selected Tino in the first round of the June amateur draft. He was the fourteenth player selected in the entire country. Another amazing honor was bestowed on Tino that same spring. He was chosen to play on the United States Olympic Baseball team, which would be participating in the Summer Olympics in Seoul, South Korea. Baseball was not yet a fully recognized Olympic game, so the team would be competing for a demonstration-sport medal. The Mariners did not mind and allowed Tino to play in the Olympics. It would be good experience for him.

Before going to Korea, Tino participated in other tournaments with the Olympic team in order to get ready. He was playing baseball and also got a chance to see the world. One of the more memorable tournaments was the World Amateur Championships held in Parma, Italy. Tino showed the world just how good he was. He was named the Most Valuable Player (MVP) of the tournament. He batted an incredible .413 (which means he had better than four hits every ten times at bat), hit four home runs, and drove in 18 runs, leading the U.S. team to victory.

The summer before the Olympics were to begin, the U.S. Olympic team played in several tournaments and played against such world-renowned powerhouse teams as Cuba and Japan. They also competed against very good teams from Puerto Rico, the Dominican Republic, and Venezuela. Tino was facing the best competition in the world outside the major leagues.

Just a year before, Tino had the privilege of being chosen to represent the United States on the Pan-American baseball team. The Pan-Am Games is a tournament between most of the Caribbean nations as well as North and South America. The United States lost the gold medal to Cuba.

The U.S. Olympic team consisted of some of the best American college baseball players ever to play the game. The pitching staff featured future major-league superstars Jim Abbot and Andy Benes, Ben McDonald and Pat Combs. The infield was also solid with Tino at first base, Ty Griffin at second, and future All-Star Robin Ventura at third. The players were excited to put their minor-league careers on hold for a few months to represent their country.

"I never played on a team like this," said Benes, a University of Evansville pitcher. The San Diego Padres made him the first player chosen in the draft. "It's important to take advantage of it. I don't think that you'll remember your first minor-league summer as much."

Tino kept a low profile and just tried to fit in with his teammates. He often let his play on the field do his talking for him.

In between road trips, the team was based at a naval base in Millington, Tennessee. There was nothing to do there except practice playing baseball. The team traveled to Taiwan, Japan, South Korea, and Italy that summer and compiled an impressive 22-7 record by mid-August.

The U.S. team was ready for the Olympics. Unfortunately, due to political reasons, the Cuban baseball team decided not to attend the Games. The Cubans are regarded as the best amateur baseball team in the world.

The U.S. won three of their first four games, losing to Canada, but made it to the gold medal game. They faced off against Japan. The United States needed Tino to do well if they were to beat Japan.

Japan was leading 1-0 after three innings, and the Americans could not seem to hit anything hard against right-handed pitcher Takehiro Ishii. Then in the fourth inning Ventura reached base when his slow ground ball took a bad hop and skipped into right field. Tino came to bat and blasted a 410-foot home run over the center-field fence, giving the U.S. a 2-1 lead. The Americans scored another run that inning to make it 3-1.

In the next inning, Tino drove in another run when he scored Griffin with a line drive single, making it 4-1. Japan scored twice later in the game to make it 4-3. But Tino belted another home run, in the eighth inning, to solidify the victory and the gold medal. After the game, the Americans took a victory lap around the field.

"At that time, winning the gold medal was the highest point of my career, the greatest achievement as a team," Tino would say years later.

Tino finished the Olympics with the highest batting average on the American team. He batted an astonishing .474 for the tournament.

Tino's family, which always remained close, had accompanied him to South Korea to watch him play in the Olympics. Winning the gold medal in front of his dad was one of the biggest thrills in his life. Tino was hoping that the next thrill would be to have his father there when he finally made it to the major leagues.

The next spring, Tino reported to the minor leagues for his first experience in professional baseball. Once again, he did well. In fact, he became such a feared hitter that he led the Eastern League with 13 intentional walks. Many times, a team will choose to walk a good hitter so that he will not have an opportunity to drive in a run. Tino also led all first basemen in the Eastern League with 1,348 total chances and 106 double plays.

Tino hit 13 home runs and 29 doubles to go along with a respectable .257 batting average that season. He also struck out only 54 times in a league-leading 509 at-bats.

After the season, Tino returned home to Tampa to spend the off-season with his family. He was very happy because he had been told that he had been promoted to the Calgary ball club of the Pacific Coast League. This was Seattle's top minor-league team. Tino was now one step away from the major leagues.

Then tragedy struck the Martinez family. Three days before Christmas in 1989, Rene Sr. began to complain of headaches. Over the next few days, the pain continued to get worse and worse. The headache became so painful that Rene Sr. could not get out of bed. On New Year's Eve, Sylvia checked her husband into a hospital. The doctors discovered a brain tumor and wanted to operate right away, but it would be risky. The doctors operated on January 3; Rene died the following day. He was only 48 years old.

Tino's first major-league game was August 20, 1990. Though he started off strong, he tried too hard and fell into an early slump.

a taste of the major leagues. Usually, major-league teams will call up their top prospects near the end of the baseball season in order to give them a little experience.

Tino's first major-league game was August 20, 1990. The Mariners were facing the Texas Rangers and their ace pitcher, Bobby Witt. That season, Witt posted a 17-10 record and struck out 221 batters. He could throw extremely hard.

Tino got his major-league career off to a flying start. He singled in his first at-bat. In fact, Tino got three hits that night, helping the Mariners to a win and giving Seattle fans a glimpse of what he could do.

The major leagues must have seemed easy for Tino, because the next night he drove in the first two runs of his major-league career. But then he seemed to get overpowered by experienced big-league pitchers. He started trying too hard, trying to impress everybody. He fell into a terrible slump. Tino played on and off at first base for the next month and collected only one hit in his next 29 at-bats. But he did not give up. He practiced harder and kept working on his swing.

By mid-September, Tino seemed to have worked out of his slump and hit safely in five straight games, getting six base hits over those games. The Mariners rewarded him by starting him for the last nine games of the season. Tino's final numbers during his first taste of the major leagues were not too impressive. He batted .221 with no home runs and only five RBIs.

Later that year, Tino married his old sweetheart, Marie. Tino wanted to have children right away. He hoped to be as good a father as Rene Sr. had been to him.

Tino would start the next season at Calgary once again. It is not uncommon for players to play several seasons at the AAA level to get ready for the majors.

Tino was gaining a reputation as being a good player and a good person.

"There really are no negatives about Tino," said Calgary manager Tom Jones. "He's a tremendous human being in addition to being a tremendous player."

The Mariners farm director and former major-league pitcher Jim Beattie agreed. "His work ethic is tremendous. You see a lot of players who have talent and potential, but you don't see them putting in the extra time to be a great player. You see it in Tino," Beattie said.

Tino had another great year. He was voted Most Valuable Player of the Pacific Coast League after batting .326 with 18 home runs and 86 runs batted in. Tino not only had home-run power, he had extra-base-hit power. He pounded 34 doubles and five triples. There was talk about having Tino switch to the outfield since the Mariners already had two pretty good first basemen in Alvin Davis and Pete O'Brien.

"I've played a little outfield and some third base," Tino said. "I'll play wherever they want me to."

Tino's great hitting would not keep him out of the Mariners lineup.

Tino was recalled by Seattle on August 22 and has been in the majors ever since. On August 26, Tino hit his first home run. He belted a 395-foot homer into the third deck in right field at Seattle's Kingdome Stadium off Milwaukee Brewers pitcher Julio Machado.

But once again Tino struggled. He played 29 games at first base and was the designated hitter in five games. He batted only .205 with four home runs and nine RBIs. He also struck out 24 times in only 112 at-bats. Even though Tino had displayed little of his ability, he was awarded the starting first base job for the 1992 season. Tino would not learn any more by playing another year at Calgary. He would have to learn while in the major leagues. One of Tino's main goals for the 1992 season was to avoid any prolonged batting slumps. He knew the first base job was his, and he wanted to be consistent.

Tino did not wait long to show Seattle fans that he deserved the job. He hit a home run on opening night, April 6, off the Texas Rangers' tough left-handed

On April 25, 1992, Tino belted his first career grand slam against the California Angels.

pitcher Floyd Bannister. A few weeks later, on April 25, Tino belted his first career grand slam against California pitcher Joe Grahe. By the All-Star break, Tino was one of the most consistent and reliable Seattle Mariners. He batted .255 with seven home runs and 37 RBIs. He was halfway to his goal.

Tino did not slump during the second half of the season either. He batted .259 with nine home runs and 29 RBIs. His 16 home runs gave Seattle a real power threat to go along with superstar Ken Griffey Jr.

That summer, Tino and Marie were blessed with the birth of a daughter, Olivia. She was born on August 10, 1992.

Tino got off to a super start in the 1993 season. He repeated his opening-day heroics when he homered against Toronto pitcher Mike Timlin. He set a club record with five walks on April 14 at Toronto. He also hit six home runs for the month of May. By the time the All-Star break rolled around, Tino was already well ahead of his previous year's pace. He had 13 home runs and 44 RBIs. He continued his hot hitting in July when he batted .303 with four home runs and 18 RBIs. But, Tino's season would be cut short. He suffered a painful knee injury while running the bases during a game at Kansas City on August 9. He would miss the remainder of the season.

Disappointment and pain were mixed with happiness, however, as Marie gave birth to their son, T.J., (Tino, Jr.) who was born a day later. Ironically, T.J. was born on the same date as his sister, Olivia.

Tino was now a bonafide major-league player. He had fulfilled his dream and the dream of his father. It still caused him pain to talk about his father, but he knew that Rene would have been proud of him.

"It bothers me that he was not here to see me make it to the majors," Tino said. "Although I know that he's watching, I wish he was here. I think he knows I made it. He really believed and I really believed. I don't think that he was just saying that. I think he meant it from the inside."

Tino worked hard rehabilitating his knee so that he would be ready for the 1994 season. Although he was in great shape, Tino started the season in a horrible slump. Through May 19, he was batting a miserable .189 with only three home runs. But then just like that, Tino snapped out of it. On May 20 he started a three-game home-run streak that seemed to wake up his bat. On June 28, Tino began a 13-game hitting streak that raised his batting average 29 points.

In early August, Tino put together another three-game home-run streak and even knocked in a career-high six runs on August 8 at Texas. He finished the season strong: over his last 32 games of the season, he hit .353 with 11 home runs and 27 RBIs. Tino was also proud of the fact that he was now considered one of the best fielders in the league. He finished second in fielding percentage, trailing only Don Mattingly.

Even though Tino was a serious power hitter, he said, "I don't really consider myself to be a power hitter. I try to hit line drives. What I try to do is just keep my line drive mentality, my line drive focus, hitting the ball to all fields. And when I get ahold of one, obviously I can hit it out."

The Seattle Mariners were improving as Tino and some of their other younger players improved. Tino was on the verge of stardom.

CHAPTER 5
Tino the Superstar

When the 1995 season rolled around, Tino was becoming a real fan favorite in Seattle. The Mariners were becoming an American League powerhouse with hitters like Ken Griffey Jr., Edgar Martinez, Tino Martinez, and Jay Buhner. The fans in Seattle really appreciated the attitude that Tino brought with him every day to the ballpark. He had to work hard for everything he accomplished. He appreciated the fans as much as they appreciated him.

"I am a working-class ballplayer. I don't think I'm physically gifted with speed or a great arm or all the five-star tools that the superstars of the game possess," he said. "I have to work hard at my hitting and fielding to be successful and to stay successful." (Certain ballplayers are known as five-star players because they have above-average speed, power, fielding, throwing, and batting skills.)

Tino got off to a good start in 1995 and never let up. He had his best season yet. In early July, Tino was voted the American League Player of the Week for July 3–July 9 when he hit .393 with four homers and 11 RBIs.

A few weeks earlier, Tino showed the fans at Yankee stadium what the Mariner home-run hitter was

Tino hit a 2-run homer in the 5th inning against the New York Yankees, 10/6/95.

all about. On June 11, he became just the eighth player since 1973 to homer into the bleachers in center field at Yankee Stadium. He belted that shot off left-handed pitcher Bob MacDonald. He also punished the Yankees during a three-game sweep in Seattle early in the season, including hitting two homers and driving in five runs during the final game, an 11-9 Seattle victory.

That summer, Tino was treated to another first. He was chosen to play in his first All-Star Game. Tino was a late replacement for the injured Oakland star Mark McGwire. Other highlights for Tino that season included two grand slams and a 14-game hitting streak. During that span Tino hit .333.

Tino finished the season with great numbers. He batted .293 with 31 home runs and 111 RBIs. He also hit 35 doubles.

The Mariners made the playoffs. They would participate in the first ever Wild Card series, which was against the New York Yankees. Tino had always done well against his future team. Through 1995, Tino had a .322 career average against the Yanks, including 13 home runs and 32 RBIs. In 1995 he hit .319 against them with five homers and 13 runs batted in. He helped the Mariners win nine of 13 regular-season games. Now it was time for the playoffs.

It was a great series. The Yankees jumped out to a two-games-to-one lead in the best-of-five series, but the Mariners would not give up. With hitters like Tino, Griffey, Buhner, and Edgar Martinez, the Mariners stormed back. They tied the series and then both clubs braced for what was sure to be a classic game five.

Yankee starter David Cone tired late in the game and allowed the Mariners to tie the score 5-5. The game went into extra innings. The Mariners won 6-5, taking the series.

Tino hit .409 for the series. He gathered nine hits in five games, belting a homer and driving in five runs.

The Mariners were set to face the American League powerhouse Cleveland Indians. The Indians had ripped through the American League in 1995 and were heavy favorites to win the best-of-seven series from Seattle. The Mariners would need a strong series from their star sluggers.

The Mariners jumped out to an improbable two-games-to-one lead in the series despite a team-wide batting slump. Edgar Martinez was held hitless for the first three games, and Tino had only one hit during that span.

"I don't think that we've had three games all year where Edgar and Tino have been stopped," Piniella said.

The slump would eventually catch up to the team, and the Indians won a hard-fought series in six games. They went on to lose to the Atlanta Braves in the World Series.

Tino batted only .136 in the series with a paltry three hits in 22 plate appearances. All three hits were singles, and he did not drive in a run. But, even though the Mariners lost the series, there was great hope for the future of this young, talented team.

However, that winter, the owners of the team were concerned about the club's payroll, which was the largest in team history. Tino would be eligible for arbitration in the spring, and the Mariners knew that he would command a lot of money. Arbitration is a process that major-league players and owners use to determine the rate of pay for players who are not eligible to become free agents yet and who cannot come to a salary agreement. With the great season that Tino had just had, he was sure to win a lot of money.

The Mariners already had Edgar Martinez, Ken Griffey Jr., and pitcher Randy Johnson locked up with big contracts. They would not be able to afford Tino. The owners put him on the market. The Yankees were immediately interested and made a deal for the lefty slugger.

"In a perfect world we don't make this trade," said Seattle general manager Woody Woodward. "We would keep the whole team intact and move on. That's not reality. The reality was, to get our budget we had to make a move."

Lou Piniella was upset by the trade, but he also understood the need for the move. "Tino was a player that I enjoyed managing," he said. "You get attached, even though you're not supposed to. This is something the organization had to do."

Seattle's loss was New York's gain. Tino replaced Don Mattingly at first base, and, after getting off to a slow start for the Yankees, he showed the New York fans that he was a powerful threat. Along with out-fielders Paul O'Neill and Bernie Williams, Tino helped lead the Yankees to the Eastern Division crown. The Yankees had the best record in baseball.

"I was happy about the trade because I knew that I was going to a great team," Tino said. "I was fortunate to get traded to a team that had made the play-offs the year before and had a good chance to go back again."

On a personal level, Tino relished the idea of playing in New York and did not shy away from the limelight. He moved his family to Tenafly, New Jersey, which was, ironically, where Don Mattingly lived.

"Guys who struggle here are guys who don't want to be here," Tino said. "My wife and I both love New York and want to be here."

Tino became popular with the fans and the New York media but wanted to keep his focus on baseball.

Tino has become a popular player for the New York Yankees. He appreciates his fans as much as they appreciate him.

He denied requests to appear on talk shows because he wanted to concentrate on his job. Tino spends most of his free time with his family. He likes taking the family to Broadway plays and musicals. His children especially loved *Beauty and the Beast*. Tino also likes to attend New York Knicks basketball games with his wife and kids. Hr has said that he feeds off the incredible energy in New York and turns it into positive energy for himself.

In 1996, the Yankees were favored to make it to the World Series, but first they would have to play the tough Texas Rangers in the opening round of the playoffs.

The Yankees took the series from Texas in only four games. They were led by Puerto Rican superstar Bernie Williams. Tino batted a respectable .267 in the series, including belting a pair of doubles and scoring four runs.

The next obstacle for the Yankees on their quest to go to the World Series would be the Baltimore Orioles. The Orioles boasted a tremendous pitching staff led by Mike Mussina. They also had Brady Anderson, who finished the season with more than 50 home runs.

At this time, something started happening to Tino that had never happened before in his career. He started getting tired. He had spent so much energy trying to work himself out of the early-season slump that he was exhausted. He had spent months taking extra batting practice and hitting off the tee to get himself on track. "I was grinding every single day, and it took a toll," he said.

Tino faltered in the playoffs. Against Baltimore he had only three singles and one double in 22 at-bats for a .182 batting average. More importantly, he did not drive in a single run.

Even without Tino's help, the Yankees beat Baltimore in five games and were ready to face the National League's best team and defending world champs, the Atlanta Braves. There were rumors, however, that if Tino did not start hitting, Yankee manager Joe Torre might have to bench him.

The Yankees were beaten by the Braves in the first two games and Tino was mired in a terrible slump. Torre made a tough decision and decided to use Cecil Fielder, the usual designated hitter, at first base. This allowed Torre to use other players such as Tim Raines and Jim Leyritz as designated hitters.

Tino was very upset that he would not be playing. "I told him that he wasn't playing and I knew he was angry," Torre said. "He didn't say a word."

Even though he was angry, Tino knew that he would have to be ready as a pinch hitter or as a substi-

Tino swings his bat as Kansas City Royals catcher MacFarlane remains at the ready.

tute in case someone got hurt. Tino is a good team player.

"I was hurt, deeply hurt," Tino said. "I had busted my butt day in and day out and never asked for a day off all year. I was definitely mad, but I kept it to myself. I walked back to my locker and, after a minute, told myself, 'Okay, be ready to come off the bench. You don't want to come in and do something bad because you weren't ready to play.' I never have talked to Joe about it."

Tino's anger did not last long as the Yankees won the next four games of the Series to become world champions. Even though he did not play well in the Series, Tino and his teammates knew that they had made it that far because of Tino's solid play all season. Tino was not angry anymore. In fact, two months later, he sent Torre a Christmas present. He sent him two boxes of expensive cigars.

Tino is generally a solid player. Sometimes he falters in playoff games.

CHAPTER 6
Breakout

Tino had won an Olympic gold medal, was part of a World Series championship team, and had been named to a few All-Star teams. He had a beautiful wife and three lovely children. He was also rich beyond his dreams. But Tino was still missing one thing in his career.

Although he had posted impressive numbers for the last two seasons, Tino was still waiting for his breakout season, a season in which he would fulfill all his potential and become one of baseball's best players.

Tino was usually a very slow starter and many years had poor numbers for the month of April. But he was still smarting from his poor World Series performance, so he was determined to start the 1997 season quickly. Tino came to spring training relaxed and determined.

A determined Tino meant that the rest of the American League was in trouble. He set the major-league record for the most RBIs for the month of April when he drove in 34 runs. For the five previous Aprils of his career, Tino had a total of only 45 RBIs.

Tino showed everyone just how ready he was only a few days into the season. On April 2, Tino punished his former Seattle teammates when he belted three home runs and drove in seven as the Yanks routed the Mariners 16-2. Tino also scored five runs in the game.

"I couldn't believe I did it," Tino said after the game. "Everything I swung at, I just hit it perfect. I just made good swings."

Tino hit a three-run homer in the first inning, a two-run shot in the third inning, and a solo home run in the fifth inning. All three home runs came against pitcher Scott Sanders. Tino had a few chances to become the 13th player in major-league history to hit four homers in a game, but then he singled, walked, grounded out, and struck out. All in all it was a pretty good day for the Yankee slugger.

Pretty soon it was obvious to everyone in baseball that Tino could not be stopped. If there were men on base, chances were he was going to drive them home. He finished April with eight homers.

"There's something about Tino," said Yankee teammate Paul O'Neill. "He always gets big base hits."

He kept getting base hits and kept driving in runs. It was clear that Tino, who just a season before had had a hard time winning Yankee fans to his side, was now the most popular player on the team. By early July, Yankee fans were chanting "MVP! MVP!" every time Tino stepped to the plate.

Newspapers and television stations wanted to follow Tino around to see what had changed for the Yankee slugger. How had he become so great?

"Nothing has changed for me," a smiling Tino said. "I don't eat differently this year, I'm not lifting more weights, I haven't changed my swing."

The only thing that had changed was the way that he was crushing the baseball.

Tino's fast start also helped him and his family get really comfortable in New York. They became involved in several area charities and were always willing to lend a hand to a good cause. Tino also refused to cash in on his great start. "I don't do baseball card shows and then charge for my autograph," he said. "I don't want to cash in like that."

Many players do charge their fans for their autographs. This has been a hotly debated issue among players and card collectors. Ironically, Mattingly refused to do most baseball card shows as well because he did not think it was fair to charge his fans.

By the 1997 All-Star break Tino had smashed an astonishing 28 home runs. His previous high for an entire season had been 31. He had also driven in 78 runs. He was chosen to represent the Yankees at the annual home-run-hitting contest that takes place the day before the All-Star Game. Some of the game's best power hitters come together to whack as many balls over the fence as they can.

Tino did better than just represent the Yankees: he won the tournament. He belted 16 home runs in 41 swings.

"I just wanted to represent the Yankees and do something respectable," he said. "I really didn't expect

Tino shows off his trophy after winning the Home Run Hitting Contest at the 1997 All-Star Game. He defeated Colorado Rockies' Larry Walker in the final round to earn the title.

Tino presented his Home Run trophy and his autographed shirt to All Star Cafe on August 14, 1997.

to win. It's pretty cool. It's something I can tell my kids and grandkids, show them the trophy."

Tino was also elected by the fans to be the American League's starting first baseman in the All-Star Game. This was a surprise, since Tino beat out three very popular players for the honor, Mark McGwire, Frank Thomas, and Mo Vaughn.

Tino was hitting so well that Yankee fans stopped comparing him to Don Mattingly. Now they were comparing him to Lou Gehrig, the Yankee Hall of Famer known for incredible home-run and RBI totals.

In early August, Tino hit two home runs, including a grand slam to help the Yankees beat the Chicago White Sox and their good left-handed pitcher Wilson Alvarez. It gave Tino 33 home runs for the season, his fourth multiple-home-run game, and a league-leading 90 runs batted in. Newspapers began publishing charts comparing Tino's season with Gehrig's 1934 season. That year Gehrig hit 49 homers and drove in 165 runs.

"I got off to a fast start in April and kept swinging good," Tino said. "I'm not surprised at the way I'm playing. I just hope it keeps going."

But as usual, Tino was more interested in helping his teammates win than in his individual numbers.

"Last season was great, winning a World Series, and this year we're in the race again. That makes it fun. The home runs are just something that's going on. Winning is what's made this year so much fun," he said.

Tino went through the entire year with only a minor slump. He finished the season with an astonishing 44 home runs and 141 runs batted in. He batted .296 and scored 96 runs. He helped the Yankees to their third consecutive playoff appearance.

The Yankees were heavy favorites to repeat as world champions but were upset by the Cleveland Indians in the first round of the playoffs. Once again Tino and his teammates fell into a batting slump for the entire Series. Only Paul O'Neill seemed to be able to hit the ball.

When the 1998 baseball season started, everyone expected the Yankees and Tino to have another great season. After all, they had won the World Series in 1996 and made the playoffs in 1997. They boasted a lineup that featured sluggers like Tino, Bernie Williams, Derek Jeter, Paul O'Neill and Darryl Strawberry. They also had great pitchers like David Wells, David Cone, and Mariano Rivera.

The Yankees did not disappoint. Despite getting off to an 0-4 start, the Yankees took control of first place in mid-April and never looked back. Tino hit his first home run of the season on April 10 against Oakland and drove in a whopping five runs. That started a six-game stretch in which Tino drove in at least two runs a game.

The Yankees were a powerhouse team that just breezed through the regular season. They finished with an American League record 114 wins. Tino had another great season. He batted .281 with 28 home runs and 123 runs batted in.

The Yankees swept the Rangers in three games in the first round of the playoffs. Then they beat the Indians in a five-game series. Although the Yankees were having an easy time in the playoffs, their big hitters, Tino and Bernie Williams were not hitting well. It was the third post-season in a row that Tino was in a slump. People in New York were wondering whether Tino had what it took to be a big time player, especially in clutch situations.

But Tino erased everyone's doubts in the first game of the World Series against the tough San Diego Padres. The Yankees were down by three runs in the 7th inning when second baseman Chuck Knoblauch belted a three-run homer to tie the game. But that was not all. Four batters later, Tino was up with the bases loaded. He worked the count in his favor as the Yan-

A smiling Tino looks forward to many more years in the major leagues.

kee Stadium fans waited for Tino to finally do something good.

He did not let the fans down. Tino turned on a high fastball from left-handed pitcher Mark Langston and smacked a grand slam home run into the second deck in right field. Tino raised his fist and smiled as he rounded the bases. He finally came through in a big game. The Yankees went on to win the game and Tino was the hero.

Tino got three big hits in the second game of the Series as the Yankees cruised to an easy win. He was no longer in a slump. The Yankees went on to sweep the Padres in four games to become the World Series champions. Some people regard the 1998 Yankees to be the greatest team to ever play the game. When historians look back, they would find that Tino was one of the main sluggers and great fielders on one of the top teams of all time.

Life has pretty much stayed the same for the Martinez family. Tino's mother, Sylvia, still teaches school and still lives on Kathleen Street; his brother, Rene, still works at a bank; and his grandfather Constantino, at the age of 79, still runs his cigar factory. Sometimes Tino jokes that he will send his son T.J. to work at the factory, unloading crates of tobacco in the Florida heat.

The Yankees and their fans will be able to cheer for number 24, Tino Martinez, for years to come. And one day the pressure will be on another first baseman who will be trying to fill Tino's shoes. It will not be easy.

Tino smacked a grand slam home run in the first game of the 1998 World Series.

MAJOR LEAGUE STATS

YR	TEAM	G	AB	R	H	2B	3B	HR	RBI	BB	AVG
1990	Sea	24	68	4	15	4	0	0	5	9	.221
1991	Sea	36	112	11	23	2	0	4	9	11	.205
1992	Sea	136	460	53	118	19	2	16	66	42	.257
1993	Sea	109	408	48	108	25	1	17	60	45	.265
1994	Sea	97	329	42	86	21	0	20	61	29	.261
1995	Sea	141	519	92	152	35	3	31	111	62	.293
1996	NYA	155	595	82	174	28	0	25	117	68	.292
1997	NYA	158	594	96	176	31	2	44	141	75	.296
1998	NYA	142	531	92	149	33	1	28	123	61	.281
1999	NYA	159	589	95	155	27	2	28	105	69	.263
TOTALS		1157	4205	615	1156	225	11	213	798	471	.260

CHRONOLOGY

1967 Born December 7
1985 Graduated from Jefferson High School
      Enrolled at the University of Tampa
1988 Was part of the United States Gold Medal Olympic Baseball Team
      Was chosen in first round of baseball draft by the Seattle Mariners in June
1990 Named USA Today's Minor League Player of the Year
1991 Named Pacific Coast League Most Valuable Player
      Was called up by Seattle on August 22
1992 Hit a home run on opening day, April 6
1993 Hit a home run on opening day, April 6
1995 Set Mariners record for home runs by a first baseman with 31
      Traded to the New York Yankees on December 7
      Ranked first in fielding among American League first basemen
1996 Won his first world series as Yankees beat the Braves
1997 Led the American League in sacrifice flies and second in home runs
1998 Drove in more than 100 runs for the third straight season
      Helped Yankees win world series with big grand slam
1999 Slid below league average in many areas, though he did knock in 105 runs

INDEX